Preston Lee's
Intermediate ENGLISH

Lesson 1 - 20

For Ukrainian Speakers

GW00482251

This book belongs to

_____

CONTENTS

Lesson 1: My family

моя родина

Learn the words

1. **mother**
   мати
2. **grandmother**
   бабуся
3. **sister**
   сестра
4. **baby sister**
   молодша сестра
5. **aunt**
   тітка

6. **father**
   батько
7. **grandfather**
   дідусь
8. **brother**
   брат
9. **baby brother**
   молодший брат
10. **uncle**
    дядько

Learn the verb

see – seeing – saw – seen бачити

I will **see** this movie with my brother.

I am **seeing** this movie with my brother.

I **saw** this movie with my brother.

I had **seen** this movie with my brother.

Learn the phrasal verb

Spend time with

Meaning: To do something with someone for a period of time.

I'll be spending time with my uncle this weekend.

Words: Write the missing letters

1. m_ _h_ _

2. g_a_dm_t_e_

3. s_s_e_

4. ba_y si_t_ _

5. a_n_

6. f_t_e_

7. g_a_df_t_e_

8. _r_t_e_

9. _a_y b_o_h_r

10. u_c_ _

Verbs: Past, Present or Future?

1. We haven't seen our uncle for a long time.
☐ Past ☐ Present ☐ Future

2. Next weekend, I will see my grandfather at his house.
☐ Past ☐ Present ☐ Future

3. My brother and I saw the sunset at the beach yesterday.
☐ Past ☐ Present ☐ Future

Phrasal Verbs: Unscramble the sentences

1. uncle / likes / spending / time / He / his / with

_____

2. We / week / families / time / with / our / spent / last / some

_____

3. her / often / spends / She / with / time / grandmother

_____

Sentence Pattern 1

Who will you be spending time with this weekend?

I'll be spending time with my <u>grandmother</u> this weekend.

Will you be spending time with your <u>father</u> this weekend?

A: Yes, I will be.

B: No, I'll be spending time with my <u>uncle</u>.

Sentence Pattern 2

How many <u>brother</u>s do you have?

I have <u>two</u> brothers.

Do you have any <u>sister</u>s?

A: Yes, I have <u>one</u> sister.

B: No, I don't have any sisters.

Sentence Pattern 3

Whose room is this one?

This is my <u>grandfather</u>'s room.

Is this your <u>aunt</u>'s room?

A: Yes, it is.

B: No, it's my <u>baby sister</u>'s room.

Sentence Pattern 1

Who _____ you be _____ time _____ this _____?

I'll _____ spending _____ with my _____ this weekend.

Will _____ be _____ time with your _____ this _____?

A: Yes, _____ will _____.

B: _____, I'll be _____ time _____ _____ mother.

Sentence Pattern 2

How _____ sisters _____ you _____?

_____ have _____ _____.

_____ you _____ any _____?

A: Yes, _____ have _____ brothers.

B: _____, I _____ have _____ _____.

Sentence Pattern 3

Whose _____ is _____ one?

This _____ my _____ room.

_____ this _____ aunt's _____?

A: Yes, _____ is.

B: _____, it's _____ _____ room.

Lesson 2: My pencil case

мій пенал

Learn the words

1. **a pencil**
   олівець
2. **an eraser**
   гумка
3. **some glue**
   клей
4. **a pencil sharpener**
   точилка
5. **some whiteout**
   коректор

6. **a pen**
   ручка
7. **a ruler**
   лінійка
8. **some tape**
   сантиметр
9. **a marker**
   маркер
10. **a crayon**
    кольоровий олівець

Learn the verb

buy – buying – bought – bought купувати

I want to **buy** a new pencil sharpener.

I will be **buying** a new pencil sharpener.

I **bought** a new pencil sharpener.

I have **bought** a new pencil sharpener.

Learn the phrasal verb

Forget to

Meaning: To not remember to do something.

I forgot to bring some whiteout.

Words: Write the vowels

1. p_nc_l

2. _r_s_r

3. gl_ _

4. p_nc_l sh_rp_n_r

5. wh_t_ _ _t

6. p_n

7. r_l_r

8. t_p_

9. m_rk_r

10. cr_y_n

Verbs: Which verb?

1. I _____ this marker at the supermarket yesterday.

2. My friend will _____ a new pencil tomorrow.

3. I have never _____ whiteout before.

4. My mom is _____ a new pencil case for me now.

Phrasal Verbs: Unscramble the sentences

1. forgotten / write / had / homework / She / to / her

_____

2. He / bring / forgot / eraser / an / to / to / the / test

_____

3. to / will / She / new / forget / get / a / pencil / probably

_____

Sentence Pattern 1

What did you forget to bring?

I forgot to bring a <u>pencil</u>.

Did you forget to bring a <u>ruler</u>?

A: Yes, I did.

B: No, I have one in my pencil case.

Sentence Pattern 2

What are you going to use?

I'm going to use <u>a marker</u>.

Are you going to use <u>an eraser</u>?

A: Yes, I am.

B: No, I'm not.

Sentence Pattern 3

How much did that <u>pen</u> cost you?

This pen cost me <u>three</u> dollars.

Did that <u>pencil</u> cost you <u>two</u> dollars?

A: Yes, it did.

B: No, it cost me <u>four</u> dollars.

Sentence Pattern 1

What _____ you _____ to _____?

_____ forgot _____ bring a _____.

Did _____ forget _____ bring _____ ruler?

A: Yes, _____ _____.

B: _____, I _____ one _____ my _____ case.

Sentence Pattern 2

What _____ you _____ to _____?

_____ going _____ use _____ marker.

_____ you _____ to _____ an _____?

A: _____, _____ am.

B: No, _____ _____.

Sentence Pattern 3

How _____ did _____ pencil _____ you?

_____ pencil _____ me _____ dollars.

_____ that _____ cost _____ two _____?

A: _____, it _____.

B: No, _____ _____ me _____ dollars.

Lesson 3: In the Classroom

в класі

Learn the words

1. **chair**
   стілець
2. **blackboard**
   класна дошка
3. **poster**
   плакат
4. **globe**
   глобус
5. **clock**
   годинник

6. **desk**
   стіл
7. **whiteboard**
   біла дошка
8. **bookshelf**
   книжкова полиця
9. **computer**
   комп'ютер
10. **book**
    книга

Learn the verb

look – looking – looked – looked дивитися

The students **look** at the computer.

The students were **looking** at the computer.

The students **looked** at the computer.

The students have **looked** at the computer.

Learn the phrasal verb

Look at

Meaning: To focus on something by seeing it.

The teacher told us to look at the poster.

Words: Unscramble the words

1. lcrbabdaok _____   6. ahicr _____

2. rotspe _____   7. oobk _____

3. htrwabdioe _____   8. sekd _____

4. olbge _____   9. ccklo _____

5. khbfoesol _____   10. oumtcerp _____

Verbs: ing or no ing?

1. The students have been ___ at the blackboard all day. ☐ looked ☐ looking

2. The teacher is ___ at the computer. ☐ looking ☐ looks

3. I have never ___ at this book before. ☐ looked ☐ looking

4. Your new classroom ___ great. ☐ looking ☐ looks

5. Stop ___ at the clock! ☐ look ☐ looking

Phrasal Verbs: Unscramble the sentences

1. at / chair / friend's / I / my / looking / was

_____

2. been / clock / looking / at / afternoon / has / all / She / the

_____

3. at / the / when / look / finished / you're / We'll / poster

_____

Sentence Pattern 1

What did the teacher tell us to look at?

The teacher told us to look at the <u>blackboard</u>.

Did the teacher tell us to look at the <u>poster</u>?

A: Yes, she did.

B: No, she told us to look at the <u>clock</u>.

Sentence Pattern 2

Where does the teacher put the <u>computer</u>?

He puts the computer <u>next to</u> the <u>desk</u>.

Does the teacher put the <u>book</u> <u>on</u> the <u>bookshelf</u>?

A: Yes, she does.

B: No, she puts the book <u>next to</u> the <u>blackboard</u>.

Sentence Pattern 3

What do you like about the classroom?

I like the <u>whiteboard</u> in the classroom.

Do you like the <u>globe</u> in the classroom?

A: Yes, I like it very much.

B: No, I don't like it at all.

Sentence Pattern 1

What _____ the _____ tell _____ to _____ at?

_____ teacher _____ us to look _____ the _____.

Did _____ teacher _____ us _____ look at _____ desk?

A: Yes, _____ _____.

B: _____, she _____ us to _____ at the _____.

Sentence Pattern 2

Where _____ the _____ put _____ _____?

_____ puts _____ computer _____ to _____ chair.

_____ the teacher _____ the globe _____ the desk?

A: _____, she _____.

B: No, _____ puts the _____ next _____ the _____.

Sentence Pattern 3

What _____ you _____ about _____ classroom?

_____ like the _____ _____ the _____.

Do _____ like _____ computer _____ the _____?

A: _____, I _____ it _____ much.

B: No, I _____ _____ it _____ _____.

Lesson 4: The weather

погода

Learn the words

1. **snowy**
   сніжна
2. **sunny**
   сонячна
3. **rainy**
   дощова
4. **windy**
   вітряна
5. **cloudy**
   марна

6. **hot**
   жарка
7. **cold**
   холодна
8. **warm**
   тепла
9. **cool**
   прохолодна
10. **freezing**
    крижана, морозна

Learn the verb

feel – feeling – felt – felt відчувати

They will **feel** warm inside the house.

They are **feeling** warm inside the house.

They **felt** warm inside the house.

They will have **felt** warm inside the house.

Learn the phrasal verb

Look like

Meaning: To appear similar or the same as something.

It looks like it's going to be freezing.

Words: Complete the words

1. c_____d

2. w_____y

3. r_____y

4. f_____g

5. su_____y

6. h_____t

7. sn_____y

8. c_____l

9. w_____m

10. c_____y

Verbs: Find the mistake

1. The snowy weather feeled cold yesterday. **Correct:** _____

2. You will feeling warm in the house. **Correct:** _____

3. It didn't felt very hot last weekend. **Correct:** _____

4. She feel freezing in her dress. **Correct:** _____

5. The sunny weather made the children felt happy. **Correct:** _____

Phrasal Verbs: Unscramble the sentences

1. a / It / looks / sunny / like / to / be / going / it's / day

_____

2. getting / like / weather / the / rainy / looking / It's / is / worse

_____

3. The / would / like / looked / weather / it / be / cool

_____

Sentence Pattern 1

What's the weather going to be like today?

It looks like it's going to be <u>rainy</u>.

Does the weather look like it's going to be <u>warm</u> today?

A: Yes, it does.

B: No, it looks like it's going to be <u>cool</u>.

Sentence Pattern 2

What kind of place would you prefer to live?

I'd prefer to live in a <u>sunny</u> place.

Would you prefer to live in a <u>cold</u> place?

A: Yes, I would.

B: No, I'd prefer to live in a <u>hot</u> place.

Sentence Pattern 3

Why did you decide to stay home?

We decided to stay home because it was <u>freezing</u>.

Did he decide to stay home because it was <u>snowy</u>?

A: Yes, that's right.

B: No, he stayed home because it was <u>windy</u>.

Sentence Pattern 1

_____ the _____ going _____ be _____ today?

It _____ like _____ going _____ be _____.

Does the _____ look like it's _____ to be _____ _____?

A: _____, it _____.

B: No, it _____ _____ it's _____ to _____ cloudy.

Sentence Pattern 2

What _____ of _____ would you _____ to _____?

_____ prefer _____ live _____ a _____ place.

_____ you _____ _____ live in _____ hot _____?

A: Yes, _____ _____.

B: _____, I'd _____ to _____ in a _____ _____.

Sentence Pattern 3

_____ did you _____ to _____ home?

We _____ to stay _____ _____ it _____ snowy.

Did _____ decide _____ stay home _____ it was _____?

A: Yes, _____ _____.

B: No, they _____ _____ because it _____ freezing.

Write the answer next to the letter "A"

A: ___ **1.** I'll be ___ time ___ my mother this weekend.

a. having, for   b. spent, with   c. spending, with   d. spend, on

A: ___ **2.** How ___ aunts ___ you have?

a. many, do   b. many, does   c. much, is   d. are, that

A: ___ **3.** ___ room is this one? This is my ___ room.

a. Who's, aunts b. Who, uncle's c. Whose, sister's d. Whose, fathers

A: ___ **4.** We ___ be ___ his family this weekend.

a. can, seen   b. will, seeing   c. may, see   d. would, saw

A: ___ **5.** She ___ never ___ glue from the supermarket.

a. is, buy   b. has, bought   c. does, buys   d. had, buying

A: ___ **6.** Did you forget ___ bring a pen? Yes, I ___.

a. too, did   b. it, forget   c. again, forgot   d. to, did

A: ___ **7.** Are you going to use ___ tape? Yes, I ___.

a. some, am   b. this, going   c. a, use   d. some, using

A: ___ **8.** This pencil sharpener ___ me seven ___.

a. costing, dollars b. costs, dollar c. costed, dollar d. cost, dollars

A: ___ **9.** The students have ___ looking ___ the whiteboard all day.

a. been, it   b. been, at   c. be, on   d. being, to

A: ___ **10.** No, the teacher ___ us to ___ at the bookshelf.

a. told, look   b. telling, looking   c. tells, looks   d. tell, look

A: ___ **11.** Does the teacher ___ the computer ___ the desk?

a. puts, next to   b. putting, on   c. put, on   d. put, next

A: ___ **12.** Do you ___ the desk in the classroom? No, I ___ like it at all.

a. liking, don't   b. like, doesn't   c. likes, not   d. like, don't

A: ___ **13.** They ___ have ___ cold for a long time.

a. would, feeling   b. will, feel   c. will, felt   d. are, felt

A: ___ **14.** Does the weather ___ like it's going to ___ snowy today?

a. look, be   b. looks, be   c. looking, being   d. looked, been

A: ___ **15.** Would you prefer to ___ in a hot place? Yes, I ___.

a. living, will   b. live, prefer   c. live, would   d. lives, do

A: ___ **16.** We ___ to ___ home because it was rainy.

a. decide, stay   b. stayed, at   c. staying, at   d. decided, stay

Answers on page 96

Lesson 5: Places

місця

Learn the words

1. **park**
   парк
2. **beach**
   пляж
3. **night market**
   нічний ринок
4. **store**
   магазин
5. **supermarket**
   супермаркет

6. **restaurant**
   ресторан
7. **swimming pool**
   басейн
8. **department store**
   універмаг
9. **cinema**
   кінотеатр
10. **gym**
   спортзал

Learn the verb

walk – walking – walked – walked ходити, гуляти

My grandmother **walks** to the supermarket by herself.

My grandmother is **walking** to the supermarket by herself.

My grandmother **walked** to the supermarket by herself.

My grandmother has **walked** to the supermarket by herself.

Learn the phrasal verb

Be about to

Meaning: To refer to something that will happen very soon.

I'm about to go to the department store now.

Words: Write the missing letters

1. p_ _k

2. be_c_

3. n_ _h_ m_r_e_

4. s_ _r_

5. s_p_ _m_ _k_ _

6. r_s_a_ _a_t

7. s_i_ _i_g p_o_

8. d_ _a_t_ _n_ _t_r_

9. c_ _e_a

10. g_ _

Verbs: Past, Present or Future?

1. They'll be walking home from the swimming pool today.
☐ Past ☐ Present ☐ Future

2. He walks to the gym each morning, even if it's cold.
☐ Past ☐ Present ☐ Future

3. We walked around the night market last night.
☐ Past ☐ Present ☐ Future

Phrasal Verbs: Unscramble the sentences

1. beach / to / to / go / They're / the / about

_____

2. leave / about / She's / swimming / the / to / pool

_____

3. He / to / about / to / go / was / the / when / called / I / gym

_____

Sentence Pattern 1

When are you going to the <u>park</u>?

I'm about to go to the park now.

Are you going to the <u>swimming pool</u> soon?

A: Yes, I'm about to go there now.

B: No, I'm about to go to the <u>store</u>.

Sentence Pattern 2

Where was he when you called him?

He was at the <u>cinema</u> when I called.

Was she at the <u>supermarket</u> when you called her?

A: Yes, she was.

B: No, she was at the <u>gym</u>.

Sentence Pattern 3

What time do you want to meet at the <u>restaurant</u>?

Let's meet at <u>two</u> o'clock at the restaurant.

Do you want to meet at the <u>park</u> at <u>ten</u> o'clock?

A: Yes, that sounds good.

B: No, let's meet at the <u>beach</u> instead.

Sentence Pattern 1

When _____ you _____ to _____ _____ store?

I'm _____ to _____ _____ the department _____ now.

_____ you _____ to the _____ soon?

A: Yes, _____ about _____ go _____ now.

B: _____, I'm _____ to _____ to _____ night _____.

Sentence Pattern 2

Where _____ she _____ you _____ her?

_____ was _____ the _____ when _____ called.

_____ he at _____ _____ when you _____ _____?

A: _____, _____ was.

B: No, _____ was _____ the _____ pool.

Sentence Pattern 3

What _____ do _____ want to _____ at the _____?

Let's _____ at four _____ at _____ gym.

Do you _____ to _____ at the _____ at _____ o'clock?

A: _____, that _____ good.

B: No, _____ meet _____ the restaurant _____.

Lesson 6: Sports

спорт

Learn the words

1. **basketball**
   баскетбол
2. **soccer**
   футбол
3. **badminton**
   бадмінтон
4. **golf**
   гольф
5. **hockey**
   хокей

6. **cricket**
   крикет
7. **tennis**
   теніс
8. **baseball**
   бейсбол
9. **volleyball**
   волейбол
10. **football**
    футбол

Learn the verb

play – playing – played – played грати

My friends and I **play** basketball at school.

My friends and I were **playing** basketball at school.

My friends and I **played** basketball at school.

My friends and I have **played** basketball at school.

Learn the phrasal verb

Be good at

Meaning: To do something well or with great skill.

He is very good at tennis.

Words: Write the vowels

1. b_sk_tb_ll

2. s_cc_r

3. b_dm_nt_n

4. g_lf

5. h_ck_y

6. cr_ck_t

7. t_nn_s

8. b_s_b_ll

9. v_ll_yb_ll

10. f_ _tb_ll

Verbs: Which verb?

1. He has never _____ cricket before.

2. They will be _____ volleyball at the beach with us later.

3. She _____ hockey better than anyone else on her team.

4. My brother _____ golf many times during his trip in Europe.

Phrasal Verbs: Unscramble the sentences

1. in / scoring / good / at / He's / very / hockey

_____

2. good / was / I / tennis / kid / when / a / was / at / I

_____

3. at / have / been / I / good / football / playing / never

_____

Sentence Pattern 1

Which sport is she good at?

She is very good at <u>volleyball</u>.

Is he good at <u>tennis</u>?

A: Yes, he's very good at it.

B: No, he's good at <u>badminton</u>.

Sentence Pattern 2

What does your <u>father</u> like to watch on the weekend?

He really likes to watch <u>basketball</u>.

Does your <u>aunt</u> like to watch <u>football</u> on the weekend?

A: Yes, she really does.

B: No, she prefers to watch <u>golf</u>.

Sentence Pattern 3

What will you be doing this weekend?

I'll be attending a <u>baseball</u> tournament.

Will you be attending the <u>hockey</u> tournament?

A: Yes, I will be attending it.

B: No, I won't be attending it this time.

Sentence Pattern 1

Which _____ is _____ good _____?

He _____ very _____ at _____.

_____ she _____ at _____?

A: _____, she's _____ good _____ it.

B: No, _____ good _____ _____.

Sentence Pattern 2

What _____ your _____ like to _____ on the _____?

He _____ likes _____ _____ cricket.

Does _____ brother like to watch _____ on _____ weekend?

A: Yes, _____ really _____.

B: No, he _____ to _____ _____.

Sentence Pattern 3

What _____ you _____ doing _____ weekend?

_____ be _____ a _____ tournament.

Will _____ be _____ the soccer _____?

A: _____, I _____ be attending _____.

B: No, I _____ be _____ it _____ time.

Lesson 7: At the zoo

в зоопарку

Learn the words

1. **monkey**
   мавпа
2. **lion**
   лев
3. **tiger**
   тигр
4. **rhino**
   носоріг
5. **bear**
   ведмідь

6. **penguin**
   пінгвін
7. **giraffe**
   жирафа
8. **elephant**
   слон
9. **kangaroo**
   кенгуру
10. **crocodile**
    крокодил

Learn the verb

like – liking – liked – liked любити

My baby brother really **likes** the giraffe.

My baby brother is really **liking** the giraffe.

My baby brother really **liked** the giraffe.

My baby brother would have really **liked** the giraffe.

Learn the phrasal verb

Look forward to

Meaning: To be excited about something in the future.

I'm looking forward to seeing a kangaroo.

Words: Unscramble the words

1. leneahtp _____

2. rtgie _____

3. rfaigfe _____

4. oinl _____

5. inengpu _____

6. nyomek _____

7. aorgakon _____

8. nrohi _____

9. oirlcedco _____

10. ebar _____

Verbs: ing or no ing?

1. My brother really ____ seeing the monkey this morning. ☐ liked ☐ liking

2. The penguins really ____ eating that kind of fish. ☐ like ☐ liking

3. The class has been ____ the trip to the zoo so far. ☐ like ☐ liking

4. That old bear ____ sleeping for most of the day. ☐ likes ☐ liking

5. The crocodile is ____ its new home. ☐ like ☐ liking

Phrasal Verbs: Unscramble the sentences

1. to / to / look / forward / the / They / always / going / zoo

_____

2. I / penguins / the / to / think / forward / are / looking / eating

_____

3. forward / a / She's / looking / to / really / seeing / tiger

_____

Sentence Pattern 1

Which animal are you looking forward to seeing?

I'm looking forward to seeing a <u>lion</u>.

Are you looking forward to seeing a <u>giraffe</u>?

A: Yes, I am.

B: No, I'm looking forward to seeing a <u>rhino</u>.

Sentence Pattern 2

What was your favorite animal at the zoo?

My favorite animal was the <u>elephant</u>.

Was your favorite animal at the zoo the <u>monkey</u>?

A: Yes, the monkey was my favorite animal.

B: No, my favorite animal was the <u>kangaroo</u>.

Sentence Pattern 3

How many <u>tiger</u>s does the zoo have?

The zoo has <u>two</u> tigers.

Does the zoo have any <u>bear</u>s?

A: Yes, the zoo has <u>three</u> bears.

B: No, the zoo doesn't have any bears.

Sentence Pattern 1

Which _____ are _____ looking _____ to _____?

I'm _____ forward _____ seeing a _____.

_____ you _____ forward _____ seeing _____ elephant?

A: _____, I _____.

B: No, _____ looking _____ to _____ a _____.

Sentence Pattern 2

What _____ your _____ animal _____ the _____?

_____ favorite _____ was the _____.

Was _____ favorite _____ at _____ zoo the _____?

A: _____, the rhino _____ my _____ animal.

B: No, _____ favorite animal _____ the _____.

Sentence Pattern 3

How _____ rhinos _____ the _____ have?

_____ zoo _____ five _____.

_____ the _____ have _____ monkeys?

A: Yes, _____ zoo _____ eight _____.

B: _____, the _____ _____ have _____ monkeys.

Lesson 8: Colors

кольори

Learn the words

1. **red**
   червоний
2. **blue**
   синій
3. **orange**
   помаранчевий
4. **pink**
   рожевий
5. **black**
   чорний

6. **yellow**
   жовтий
7. **green**
   зелений
8. **purple**
   фіолетовий
9. **brown**
   коричневий
10. **white**
    білий

Learn the verb

draw – drawing – drew – drawn малювати

She's going to **draw** a pink elephant.

She was **drawing** a pink elephant.

She **drew** a pink elephant.

She has **drawn** a pink elephant.

Learn the phrasal verb

Belong to

Meaning: To be owned by or be part of something.

That black marker belongs to Matthew.

Words: Complete the words

1. p_____e

2. o_____e

3. g_____n

4. b_____e

5. y_____w

6. w_____e

7. r_____d

8. b_____k

9. b_____n

10. p_____k

Verbs: Find the mistake

1. I have never draw a white bear before. **Correct:** _____

2. My brother is really good at draw green turtles. **Correct:** _____

3. She drawing a picture using a red crayon. **Correct:** _____

4. His younger brother always drawing with a blue pen. **Correct:** _____

5. We will be drawn some things in the red workbook. **Correct:** _____

Phrasal Verbs: Unscramble the sentences

1. to / black / That / belongs / his / car / brother

_____

2. to / blue / books / belonged / me / before / Those

_____

3. team / green / cricket / These / to / the / belong / shirts

_____

Sentence Pattern 1

Who does this <u>red</u> <u>pen</u> belong to?

That red pen belongs to <u>Jessica</u>.

Does this <u>white</u> <u>eraser</u> belong to <u>Jason</u>?

A: Yes, it does.

B: No, that white eraser belongs to <u>Emily</u>.

Sentence Pattern 2

Which <u>T-shirt</u> did he decide to get?

He decided to get the <u>green</u> one.

Did she decide to get the <u>orange</u> <u>sweater</u>?

A: Yes, she did.

B: No, she decided to get the <u>black</u> one.

Sentence Pattern 3

What color do you want the bedroom to be?

I want the bedroom to be <u>yellow</u>.

Do you want the <u>living room</u> to be <u>blue</u>?

A: Yes, that would be great.

B: No, I want it to be <u>purple</u>.

Sentence Pattern 1

Who _____ this _____ ruler _____ to?

_____ yellow _____ belongs _____ Mary.

_____ this red _____ belong _____ Peter?

A: Yes, _____ _____.

B: _____, that _____ pencil _____ to _____.

Sentence Pattern 2

_____ shirt _____ he _____ to _____?

He decided _____ get the _____ _____.

Did she _____ to _____ the _____ dress?

A: _____, she _____.

B: No, _____ decided _____ _____ the _____ one.

Sentence Pattern 3

What _____ do you _____ the kitchen to _____?

I _____ the _____ to be _____.

_____ you _____ the bathroom to _____ _____?

A: Yes, _____ would _____ great.

B: No, I _____ it _____ be _____.

Write the answer next to the letter "A"

A: ___ **1.** We've ___ to the swimming pool many times ___.

a. walk, today   b. walking, later   c. walked, soon   d. walked, before

A: ___ **2.** No, I'm ___ to ___ to the department store.

a. about, go   b. around, go   c. soon, going   d. now, gone

A: ___ **3.** Was he at the night market ___ you ___ him?

a. when, called   b. where, called   c. that, call   d. did, call

A: ___ **4.** Let's meet ___ three ___ at the swimming pool.

a. in, today   b. at, o'clock   c. on, clock   d. by, half past

A: ___ **5.** ___ have ___ playing volleyball for two hours by then.

a. They, be   b. We, being   c. We'll, been   d. They'll, be

A: ___ **6.** Which sport is he good ___? He is very ___ at golf.

a. as, good   b. for, goof   c. by, it   d. at, good

A: ___ **7.** Does your grandfather ___ to ___ baseball on the weekend?

a. likes, watch   b. like, watch   c. liking, watching   d. liked, watch

A: ___ **8.** ___ you ___ attending the football tournament?

a. Can, be   b. Are, been   c. Have, being   d. Will, be

A: ___ **9.** My sister ___ really ___ the rhinos very much this time.

a. have, liked   b. didn't, like   c. did, liked   d. been, liking

A: ___ **10.** Which animal are you ___ forward to ___?

a. look, see   b. seeing, looking   c. looking, seeing   d. see, look

A: ___ **11.** ___ was your favorite ___ at the zoo?

a. Which, animals   b. How, animals   c. What, animal   d. When, animal

A: ___ **12.** No, the zoo doesn't ___ any ___.

a. have, tiger   b. has, tiger   c. had, tigers   d. have, tigers

A: ___ **13.** ___ have ___ with many different colors today.

a. I, draw   b. We, drew   c. He, drawing   d. They, drawn

A: ___ **14.** Does this green book ___ to Kevin? Yes, it ___.

a. belong, belongs   b. belong, does   c. belongs, does   d. belonging, do

A: ___ **15.** Did he ___ to ___ the purple jacket?

a. want, gets   b. deciding, get   c. decided, getting   d. decide, get

A: ___ **16.** Do you ___ the living room to ___ yellow?

a. want, be   b. wanting, be   c. wanted, been   d. wants, being

Answers on page 96

Lesson 9: Activities

діяльность

Learn the words

1. **play piano**
   грати на піаніно
2. **read books**
   читати книги
3. **play video games**
   грати у відео ігри
4. **surf the internet**
   шукати в Інтернеті
5. **take photos**
   Фотографувати

6. **watch TV**
   дивитись телевізор
7. **sing songs**
   співати пісні
8. **study English**
   вивчати англійську
9. **play cards**
   грати в карти
10. **go shopping**
    ходити за покупками

Learn the verb

read – reading – read – read читати

My father **reads** the newspaper every day.

My father **read** the newspaper this morning.

My father is **reading** the newspaper now.

My father has **read** the newspaper today.

Learn the phrasal verb

Have fun

Meaning: To do something enjoyable.

We had fun surfing the internet.

Words: Write the missing letters

1. _la_ _i_n_
2. _ea_ _oo_s
3. p_ _y _i_e_ _a_e_
4. _u_f _h_ i_ _er_e_
5. _a_e _ho_o_

6. _a_c_ T_
7. _in_ _o_g_
8. _t_d_ E_g_i_h
9. p_a_ _a_d_
10. _o _ _o_pi_g

Verbs: Past, Present or Future?

1. Last year, he read many books about taking photos.
☐ Past ☐ Present ☐ Future

2. Right now, I'm reading a book about playing cards.
☐ Past ☐ Present ☐ Future

3. I'll be reading some novels tomorrow instead of watching TV.
☐ Past ☐ Present ☐ Future

Phrasal Verbs: Unscramble the sentences

1. We / video / have / always / playing / games / fun

_____

2. fun / had / photos / taking / She / yesterday

_____

3. fun / They / didn't / cards / playing / have / today

_____

Sentence Pattern 1

What did you do over the weekend?

We had fun <u>playing video games</u>.

Did you have fun over the weekend?

A: Yes, we had fun <u>taking photos</u>.

B: No, we had a boring weekend.

Sentence Pattern 2

What can they do while it's raining?

They can <u>surf the internet</u> while it's raining.

Can they <u>play cards</u> while it's raining?

A: Yes, they can.

B: No, they can <u>study English</u>.

Sentence Pattern 3

Who would like to <u>watch TV</u> after <u>dinner</u>?

I would like to watch TV after dinner.

Would you like to <u>read books</u> after <u>lunch</u>?

A: Yes, I would like to read books.

B: No, I would like to <u>play piano</u> instead.

Sentence Pattern 1

What _____ you do _____ the _____?

We _____ fun reading _____.

_____ you _____ fun over _____ weekend?

A: Yes, _____ had _____ taking _____.

B: _____, we _____ a _____ weekend.

Sentence Pattern 2

What _____ they _____ while _____ raining?

_____ can _____ TV _____ it's _____.

Can _____ play _____ while it's _____?

A: _____, they _____.

B: No, _____ can study _____.

Sentence Pattern 3

Who _____ like to _____ songs after dinner?

_____ would _____ to sing _____ after dinner.

_____ you like to _____ video _____ after _____?

A: Yes, _____ would _____ to play _____ games.

B: No, I _____ like to _____ the internet _____.

Lesson 10: Food & Drinks

їжа та напої

Learn the words

1. **cake**
   торт
2. **cheese**
   сир
3. **milk**
   молоко
4. **tea**
   чай
5. **soda**
   газована вода

6. **pizza**
   піца
7. **water**
   вода
8. **juice**
   сік
9. **coffee**
   кава
10. **pie**
    пиріг

Learn the verb

want – wanting – wanted – wanted хотіти

They **want** to have some coffee later.

They're **wanting** to have some coffee now.

They **wanted** to have some coffee before.

They have **wanted** some coffee all day.

Learn the phrasal verb

Organize for

Meaning: To prepare something for an event.

I have organized some pie for the occasion.

Words: Write the vowels

1. c_k_

2. ch_ _s_

3. m_lk

4. t_ _

5. s_d_

6. p_zz_

7. w_t_r

8. j_ _c_

9. c_ff_ _

10. p_ _

Verbs: Which verb?

1. They will be _____ some tea to go with their pie.

2. My uncle _____ soda every time we get pizza.

3. When I was younger, I _____ to eat cake for breakfast.

4. She has _____ a coffee since she woke up this morning.

Phrasal Verbs: Unscramble the sentences

1. some / We'll / meeting / coffee / for / our / organize

_____

2. pie / the / They / lots / of / organized / had / for / meal

_____

3. has / cake / for / She / a / organized / never / a / party

_____

Sentence Pattern 1

What have you organized for the occasion?

I have organized some <u>cake</u> for the occasion.

Have you organized any <u>coffee</u> for the occasion?

A: Yes, I've organized some.

B: No, I've organized some <u>tea</u> instead.

Sentence Pattern 2

Who was the <u>pie</u> eaten by?

The pie was eaten by <u>Helen</u>.

Was the <u>soda</u> drunk by <u>Tom</u>?

A: Yes, it was drunk by him.

B: No, the soda was drunk by <u>Jessica</u>.

Sentence Pattern 3

How much <u>cheese</u> is there in the kitchen?

There is <u>a lot of</u> cheese in the kitchen.

Is there any <u>pizza</u> in the kitchen?

A: Yes, there is a lot of pizza.

B: No, there isn't any left.

Sentence Pattern 1

What _____ you _____ for the _____?

I _____ organized some _____ for _____ occasion.

_____ you organized _____ pizza _____ the _____?

A: Yes, _____ organized _____.

B: _____, I've _____ some _____ instead.

Sentence Pattern 2

Who _____ the _____ drunk _____?

_____ juice was _____ by _____.

_____ the _____ eaten _____ Tom?

A: _____, it was _____ by _____.

B: No, _____ _____ was eaten _____ _____.

Sentence Pattern 3

How _____ water _____ there _____ the _____?

_____ is a _____ of _____ in _____ kitchen.

Is _____ any _____ in _____ kitchen?

A: Yes, _____ is _____ lot _____ coffee.

B: _____, there is _____ a _____ _____.

Lesson 11: At the fruit market

на фруктовому ринку

Learn the words

1. **orange**
   апельсин
2. **pear**
   груша
3. **watermelon**
   кавун
4. **strawberry (strawberries)**
   полуниця
5. **cherry (cherries)**
   вишня

6. **lemon**
   лимон
7. **banana**
   банан
8. **grape**
   виноград
9. **pineapple**
   ананас
10. **apple**
    яблуко

Learn the verb

need – needing – needed – needed потребувати

David **needs** some strawberries for the cake.

David is **needing** some strawberries for the cake.

David **needed** some strawberries for the cake.

David had **needed** some strawberries for the cake.

Learn the phrasal verb

Cut up

Meaning: To chop something into pieces.

Cut up ten pieces of watermelon, please.

Words: Unscramble the words

1. eppenpail _____

2. agepr _____

3. tewayrrsrb _____

4. armntwoeel _____

5. naabna _____

6. omlne _____

7. apre _____

8. ernaog _____

9. pealp _____

10. hrcrye _____

Verbs: ing or no ing?

1. My younger sister was ___ help at the fruit store. ☐ needed ☐ needing

2. He ___ some bananas to make this dessert. ☐ needs ☐ needing

3. I have never ___ much help buying pears. ☐ needed ☐ needing

4. My sick friend has been ___ to eat a lot of oranges. ☐ needed ☐ needing

5. For our party tomorrow, we ___ to buy a pineapple. ☐ need ☐ needing

Phrasal Verbs: Unscramble the sentences

1. this / cut / many / They / for / types / fruit / of / up / dessert

_____

2. up / pineapples / cut / He / any / for / didn't / us

_____

3. into / cuts / watermelon / pieces / up / She / small / the

_____

Sentence Pattern 1

How many pieces of <u>apple</u> do you want me to cut up?

Cut up <u>eight</u> pieces of apple, please.

Do you want me to cut up some pieces of <u>strawberry</u>?

A: Yes, please.

B: No, thank you.

Sentence Pattern 2

What will you be putting in the fruit salad?

I'll be putting <u>apples</u> and <u>oranges</u> in the fruit salad.

Will you be putting <u>grapes</u> in the fruit salad?

A: Yes, I will be.

B: No, I won't be.

Sentence Pattern 3

What kind of fruit smoothie is she making for us?

She's making a <u>banana</u> smoothie.

Is he making a <u>strawberry</u> smoothie for us?

A: Yes, he is.

B: No, he's making a <u>pineapple</u> smoothie.

Sentence Pattern 1

How _____ _____ of pear do you _____ me to _____ up?

_____ up _____ pieces of _____, please.

Do _____ want me to cut _____ some _____ of _____?

A: Yes, _____.

B: No, _____ you.

Sentence Pattern 2

_____ will you _____ putting _____ the _____ salad?

I'll be _____ bananas and _____ in _____ fruit _____.

Will you _____ putting _____ _____ the _____ salad?

A: _____, I _____ be.

B: No, I _____ _____.

Sentence Pattern 3

What _____ of _____ smoothie is she _____ for _____?

_____ making a _____ _____.

_____ he _____ a _____ smoothie _____ us?

A: _____, he _____.

B: No, _____ making _____ apple _____.

Lesson 12: Shapes

фігури

Learn the words

1. **square**
   квадрат
2. **circle**
   коло
3. **star**
   зірка
4. **heart**
   серце
5. **octagon**
   восьмикутник

6. **triangle**
   трикутник
7. **rectangle**
   прямокутник
8. **oval**
   овал
9. **diamond**
   ромб
10. **pentagon**
    п'ятикутник

Learn the verb

find – finding – found – found знаходити

The children will **find** things in the shape of a triangle.

The children are **finding** things in the shape of a triangle.

The children **found** things in the shape of a triangle.

The children have **found** things in the shape of a triangle.

Learn the phrasal verb

Consist of

Meaning: To be formed by or made up of something.

A rectangle consists of four sides.

Words: Complete the words

1. h_____t

2. o_____l

3. s_____r

4. r_____e

5. c_____e

6. t_____e

7. s_____e

8. p_____n

9. o_____n

10. d_____d

Verbs: Find the mistake

1. I am find a lot of mistakes in this book of shapes. **Correct:** _____

2. She didn't found the heart shape I drew for her. **Correct:** _____

3. We finds a really bright star in the sky last night. **Correct:** _____

4. He couldn't finds an easy way to draw a perfect circle . **Correct:** _____

5. They haven't finding the oval sign he talked about. **Correct:** _____

Phrasal Verbs: Unscramble the sentences

1. long / drawing / rectangles / of / many / His / consists

_____

2. squares / math / consisted / problem / of / many / That

_____

3. lots / posters / of / consist / These / shapes / of

_____

Sentence Pattern 1

How many sides does an <u>octagon</u> consist of?

An octagon consists of eight sides.

Does a <u>pentagon</u> consist of <u>five</u> sides?

A: Yes, a pentagon does.

B: I don't know.

Sentence Pattern 2

What will the <u>door</u> be in the shape of?

The door will be in the shape of a <u>rectangle</u>.

Will the cookie be in the shape of a <u>circle</u>?

A: Yes, it will be.

B: No, it will be in the shape of a <u>heart</u>.

Sentence Pattern 3

Which shape has more sides than a <u>triangle</u>?

A <u>square</u> has more sides than a triangle.

Does a <u>pentagon</u> have more sides than a <u>diamond</u>?

A: Yes, that's right.

B: I'm not sure about that.

Sentence Pattern 1

How _____ sides _____ a diamond _____ of?

A _____ consists _____ four _____.

_____ an _____ consist _____ eight _____?

A: Yes, _____ octagon _____.

B: I _____ _____.

Sentence Pattern 2

What _____ the table _____ in _____ shape _____?

The _____ will _____ in the _____ of a _____.

Will _____ cake be _____ the _____ of _____ star?

A: _____, it _____ be.

B: No, _____ will _____ in the _____ of a _____.

Sentence Pattern 3

_____ shape _____ more _____ than a _____?

A pentagon has _____ sides _____ a _____.

Does a _____ have _____ sides _____ a _____?

A: Yes, _____ _____.

B: _____ not _____ _____ that.

Write the answer next to the letter "A"

A: ___ **1.** I ___ been ___ many books this year.

a. does, do   b. haven't, reading   c. are, go   d. do, play

A: ___ **2.** What did you do over the weekend? We ___ fun ___ songs.

a. having, sing   b. have, sung   c. has, sang   d. had, singing

A: ___ **3.** ___ they go shopping ___ it's raining? Yes, they can.

a. Did, when   b. Can, while   c. Would, but   d. While, because

A: ___ **4.** ___ you like to ___ video games after lunch?

a. Would, play   b. Will, playing   c. Did, played   d. Had, played

A: ___ **5.** I ___ been ___ some water for a long time.

a. have, want   b. 'd, wanted   c. having, want   d. have, wanting

A: ___ **6.** Have you ___ any milk ___ the occasion?

a. organized, by   b. organizing, for   c. organized, for   d. organize, on

A: ___ **7.** Was the tea ___ by Mia? Yes, it was drunk by ___.

a. drunk, her   b. drunken, her   c. drank, hers   d. drink, Mia

A: ___ **8.** Is there ___ pie in the kitchen? No, there isn't any ___.

a. some, lot of   b. enough, some   c. any, left   d. more, right

A: ___ **9.** My sister really ___ some bananas ___ the fruit salad.

a. needing, on   b. needs, for   c. needed, at   d. need, by

A: ___ **10.** Do you want me to ___ up ___ pieces of pear? Yes, please.

a. cut, some   b. cutting, some   c. cut, a   d. cutted, these

A: ___ **11.** I'll be ___ cherries and grapes ___ the fruit salad.

a. putting, at   b. put, on   c. putting, in   d. puts, for

A: ___ **12.** Is he ___ a grape smoothie for us? Yes, he ___.

a. make, does   b. making, is   c. makes, makes   d. making, do

A: ___ **13.** She ___ have ___ the shapes we drew for her by now.

a. would, find   b. would like, found   c. will, found   d. just, finding

A: ___ **14.** How ___ sides does a rectangle ___ of?

a. much, contain   b. many, consist   c. many, enough   d. number, more

A: ___ **15.** Will the cookie ___ in the shape ___ a star? Yes, it will be.

a. be, of   b. being, of   c. been, of   d. be, off

A: ___ **16.** ___ a star have more sides than a square? Yes, ___ right.

a. Can, it's   b. Does, that's   c. Will, I'm   d. Would, very

Answers on page 96

Lesson 13: At the supermarket

в супермаркеті

Learn the words

1. **milk**
молоко
2. **juice**
сік
3. **meat**
м'ясо
4. **drinks**
напої
5. **vegetables**
овочі

6. **ice cream**
морозиво
7. **fruit**
фрукти
8. **bread**
хліб
9. **fish**
риба
10. **pizza**
піца

Learn the verb

get – getting – got – gotten отримувати

Who will **get** the drinks for the party?

Who is **getting** the drinks for the party?

Who **got** the drinks for the party?

Who had **gotten** the drinks for the party?

Learn the phrasal verb

Write down

Meaning: To write something on paper.

You should write vegetables down on the shopping list.

Words: Write the missing letters

1. _i_k

2. _ _i_e

3. _ea_

4. _ri_k_

5. _e_e_a_le_

6. i_e _ _ea_

7. _r_i_

8. _r_a_

9. _i_h

10. _ _z_a

Verbs: Past, Present or Future?

1. I haven't gotten fruit or vegetables yet.
☐ Past ☐ Present ☐ Future

2. I got the pizza from that new restaurant nearby.
☐ Past ☐ Present ☐ Future

3. I'll be getting bread and milk from the supermarket later.
☐ Past ☐ Present ☐ Future

Phrasal Verbs: Unscramble the sentences

1. She's / everything / at / down / we / need / the / writing / store

_____

2. fruit / should / You / down / which / we / need / write

_____

3. on / wrote / shopping / down / cream / He / the / ice / list

_____

Sentence Pattern 1

What should I write down on the shopping list?

You should write <u>vegetables</u> down on the shopping list.

Should I write <u>meat</u> down on the shopping list?

A: Yes, you should.

B: No, we have enough meat.

Sentence Pattern 2

How much <u>bread</u> do we have left?

We only have a little bread left.

Do we have any <u>milk</u> left?

A: Yes, we have some milk left.

B: No, we don't have any milk left.

Sentence Pattern 3

What would you like me to get at the supermarket?

I would like you to get some <u>fish</u>, please.

Would you like me to get some <u>bread</u> at the supermarket?

A: Yes, I would like you to get some.

B: No, we already have some.

Sentence Pattern 1

What _____ I write _____ on _____ shopping _____?

You should _____ _____ down _____ the _____ list.

_____ I write _____ down _____ the _____ list?

A: Yes, _____ _____.

B: _____, _____ have _____ bread.

Sentence Pattern 2

How _____ fruit do _____ have _____?

We _____ have _____ little _____ left.

Do _____ have _____ ice _____ _____?

A: _____, we _____ _____ _____ cream left.

B: No, we _____ have _____ ice _____ _____.

Sentence Pattern 3

What _____ you _____ me to _____ at the _____?

I would _____ you _____ get _____ juice, _____.

_____ you _____ me to get some _____ at the _____?

A: Yes, _____ would _____ you _____ get _____.

B: _____, we _____ have _____.

Lesson 14: At the ice cream shop

в кафе-морозиві

Learn the words

1. **chocolate**
   шоколад
2. **strawberry**
   полуниця
3. **mint**
   м'ята
4. **raspberry**
   малина
5. **cherry**
   вишня

6. **vanilla**
   ваніль
7. **coffee**
   кава
8. **almond**
   мигдаль
9. **caramel**
   карамель
10. **coconut**
    кокос

Learn the verb

have/has – having – had – had мати

I'll **have** the chocolate-flavored ice cream.

I'm **having** the chocolate-flavored ice cream.

I **had** the chocolate-flavored ice cream.

I've **had** the chocolate-flavored ice cream.

Learn the phrasal verb

Pick up

Meaning: To get or buy something.

Pick some raspberry ice cream up on the way.

Words: Write the vowels

1. ch_c_l_t_   6. v_n_ll_

2. str_wb_rr_   7. c_ff_ _

3. m_nt   8. _lm_nd

4. r_spb_rr_   9. c_r_m_l

5. ch_rr_   10. c_c_n_t

Verbs: Which verb?

1. She hasn't _____ raspberry ice cream before.

2. He can't remember what flavor I _____ last time.

3. Every time we get ice cream, she _____ caramel flavor.

4. Later on, we will be _____ mint ice cream with our cake.

Phrasal Verbs: Unscramble the sentences

1. up / this / cream / some / mint / ice / We / morning / picked

_____

2. will / He / up / shop / the / ice / from / cream / pick / some

_____

3. picking / ice / be / will / later / up / cherry / I / cream / some

_____

Sentence Pattern 1

What do you want me to pick up on the way?

Pick some <u>coffee</u> ice cream up on the way.

Do you want me to pick up some <u>cherry</u> ice cream on the way?

A: Sure, that would be great.

B: No, pick some <u>mint</u> ice cream up instead.

Sentence Pattern 2

Which ice cream flavor did you choose?

I chose the <u>chocolate</u> ice cream flavor.

Did you choose the <u>vanilla</u> ice cream flavor?

A: Yes, I did.

B: No, I chose the <u>caramel</u> ice cream flavor this time.

Sentence Pattern 3

What ice cream flavor does he usually get?

He usually gets <u>strawberry</u> flavor.

Does she usually get <u>raspberry</u> flavor?

A: Yes, she does.

B: No, she usually gets <u>almond</u> flavor.

Sentence Pattern 1

_____ do you _____ me to _____ up _____ the way?

Pick some _____ ice cream _____ on the _____.

Do you _____ me _____ pick up _____ mint ice _____?

A: _____, that _____ be _____.

B: No, _____ some _____ _____ cream up _____.

Sentence Pattern 2

Which _____ cream _____ did you _____?

I _____ the _____ ice _____ flavor.

Did you _____ the _____ ice _____ flavor?

A: _____, I _____.

B: No, I _____ the _____ ice cream _____ this _____.

Sentence Pattern 3

What ice _____ flavor _____ he _____ get?

_____ usually _____ _____ flavor.

_____ she _____ get _____ flavor?

A: Yes, _____ _____.

B: _____, she usually _____ vanilla _____.

Lesson 15: In the refrigerator

в холодильнику

Learn the words

1. **rice**
   рис
2. **salad**
   салат
3. **toast**
   грінки
4. **soup**
   суп
5. **dumplings**
   галушки

6. **tea**
   чай
7. **cola**
   кола
8. **eggs**
   яйця
9. **water**
   вода
10. **ice**
    лід

Learn the verb

sell – selling – sold – sold продавати

Which store **sells** free-range eggs?

Which store is **selling** free-range eggs?

Which store **sold** free-range eggs?

Which store has **sold** free-range eggs?

Learn the phrasal verb

Take out

Meaning: To remove something from inside of somewhere.

You can take the rice out of the refrigerator.

Words: Unscramble the words

1. uspo _____

2. gsge _____

3. aocl _____

4. satto _____

5. alsda _____

6. eta _____

7. rcei _____

8. eic _____

9. aewtr _____

10. ipmsgudnl _____

Verbs: ing or no ing?

1. That store nearby has never ____ any eggs. ☐ sold ☐ selling

2. My uncle's restaurant ____ a lot of rice. ☐ selling ☐ sells

3. It's easy to ____ ice on hot summer days. ☐ sell ☐ selling

4. ____ hot soup in the wintertime is a good idea. ☐ Sell ☐ Selling

5. That new shop has been ____ a lot of dumplings. ☐ selling ☐ sold

Phrasal Verbs: Unscramble the sentences

1. the / She / taken / salad / hasn't / out / yet

_____

2. cola / He / the / last / of / the / out / refrigerator / took / night

_____

3. of / want / I / you / take / to / eggs / the / out / the / bag

_____

Sentence Pattern 1

How can I help you?

You can take the <u>dumplings</u> out of the refrigerator.

Can I help you?

A: Yes, you can take the <u>soup</u> out of the refrigerator.

B: No, thanks. I'm fine.

Sentence Pattern 2

Where should I put the leftover <u>salad</u>?

You should put the leftover <u>salad</u> in the refrigerator.

Should I put the leftover <u>rice</u> in the refrigerator?

A: Yes, you should.

B: No, just leave it on the table.

Sentence Pattern 3

Who forgot to put the <u>eggs</u> in the refrigerator?

<u>Tom</u> forgot to put the eggs in the refrigerator.

Did <u>Emily</u> forget to put the <u>cola</u> in the refrigerator?

A: Yes, she did.

B: No, <u>Jason</u> forgot to do it.

Sentence Pattern 1

_____ can I _____ you?

You can _____ the _____ _____ of the _____.

Can _____ _____ _____?

A: Yes, you can _____ the _____ out _____ the _____.

B: No, _____. I'm _____.

Sentence Pattern 2

Where _____ I _____ the leftover _____?

_____ should put the _____ soup _____ the _____.

Should I put _____ leftover _____ in _____ refrigerator?

A: Yes, _____ _____.

B: No, _____ leave it _____ the _____.

Sentence Pattern 3

Who _____ to _____ the _____ in the _____?

_____ forgot _____ put the _____ in _____ refrigerator.

Did Jessica _____ to _____ the _____ in _____ _____?

A: _____, she _____.

B: No, _____ forgot _____ do _____.

Lesson 16: Jobs

профеcії

Learn the words

1. **doctor**
   лікар
2. **cook**
   повар
3. **nurse**
   медсестра
4. **police officer**
   поліцейський
5. **taxi driver**
   таксист

6. **teacher**
   вчитель
7. **farmer**
   фермер
8. **salesclerk**
   продавець
9. **firefighter**
   пожежник
10. **builder**
    будівельник

Learn the verb

work – working – worked – worked працювати

She **works** at the department store as a salesclerk.

She was **working** at the department store as a salesclerk.

She **worked** at the department store as a salesclerk.

She has **worked** at the department store as a salesclerk.

Learn the phrasal verb

Grow up

Meaning: To become an adult.

I'd like to be a police officer when I grow up.

Words: Complete the words

1. p_____ _____r

2. n_____e

3. b_____r

4. t_____ _____r

5. s_____k

6. fi_____r

7. fa_____r

8. c_____k

9. d_____r

10. t_____r

Verbs: Find the mistake

1. My cousin is work as a doctor in that hospital. **Correct:** _____

2. My father has been worked as a cook for many years . **Correct:** _____

3. Her sister will be work as a teacher next month. **Correct:** _____

4. We have never works as salesclerks before. **Correct:** _____

5. Last year, he works with a farmer growing corn. **Correct:** _____

Phrasal Verbs: Unscramble the sentences

1. a / sister / grew / My / became / and / up / doctor

_____

2. he / when / wants / be / up / farmer / a / to / grows / He

_____

3. in / another / teacher / grown / up / had / His / country

_____

Sentence Pattern 1

What would you like to be when you grow up?

I'd like to be a <u>firefighter</u> when I grow up.

Would you like to be a <u>builder</u> when you grow up?

A: Yes, I would.

B: No, I'd rather be a <u>farmer</u>.

Sentence Pattern 2

What does your <u>father</u> do for a living?

My father is a <u>doctor</u>.

Isn't your <u>aunt</u> a <u>salesclerk</u>?

A: Yes, that's right.

B: No, she's not a salesclerk anymore.

Sentence Pattern 3

What do you think is the hardest job?

I think being a <u>nurse</u> is the hardest job.

Do you think being a <u>teacher</u> is the hardest job?

A: Yes, I think it is.

B: No, I think being a <u>doctor</u> is the hardest job.

Sentence Pattern 1

What _____ you _____ to be _____ you _____ up?

I'd like to _____ a _____ when I grow _____.

Would _____ like _____ be a _____ when you _____ up?

A: _____, I _____.

B: No, _____ _____ be a _____.

Sentence Pattern 2

What _____ your _____ do _____ a _____?

_____ uncle _____ a _____.

_____ your _____ a police _____?

A: Yes, _____ _____.

B: No, he's _____ a _____ officer _____.

Sentence Pattern 3

What _____ you _____ is the _____ job?

I think _____ a _____ is _____ hardest _____.

Do you _____ being a _____ _____ the hardest _____?

A: _____, I _____ it _____.

B: No, I _____ _____ a _____ driver is the _____ job.

Write the answer next to the letter "A"

A: ___ **1.** He never ___ enough juice ___ the supermarket.

a. getting, by   b. gets, at   c. gotten, in   d. get, on

A: ___ **2.** You should ___ ice cream ___ on the shopping list.

a. has, written   b. have, wrote   c. write, down   d. have, left

A: ___ **3.** Do we have ___ fish ___? No, we don't have any fish left.

a. at all, anymore   b. some, more   c. any, left   d. leftover, for

A: ___ **4.** ___ you ___ me to get some drinks at the supermarket?

a. Will, liking   b. Would, like   c. While, liked   d. Can, like

A: ___ **5.** ___ never ___ caramel ice cream before today.

a. I'm, have   b. I've, had   c. I'll, has   d. I'd, having

A: ___ **6.** Do you want me to ___ some vanilla ice cream ___ the way?

a. pick, by   b. take, for   c. carry, at   d. pick up, on

A: ___ **7.** No, I ___ the raspberry ice cream flavor ___.

a. chose, this time   b. choose, instead   c. choosing, now   d. have, later

A: ___ **8.** What ice cream flavor ___ he ___ get?

a. did, lately   b. do, often   c. had, this time   d. does, usually

A: ___ **9.** Which restaurant ___ been ___ pork dumplings?

a. have, sold b. has, selling c. having, selling d. had, sold

A: ___ **10.** Yes, you can ___ the salad ___ the refrigerator.

a. remove, by b. take, out of c. taking, at d. taken, out of

A: ___ **11.** You should ___ the leftover rice ___ the refrigerator.

a. putting, at b. puts, next to c. put, in d. put in, by

A: ___ **12.** Did Tom ___ to put the tea in the refrigerator? Yes, he ___.

a. not, did b. forgotten, forgot c. try, does d. forget, did

A: ___ **13.** Last week, she ___ working as a nurse ___ the hospital.

a. was, at b. is, by c. has, out of d. would, on

A: ___ **14.** Would you like to ___ a cook when you grow up? Yes, I ___.

a. been, will b. being, can c. be, would d. be, like

A: ___ **15.** What does your sister ___ for a ___? My sister is a teacher.

a. work, job b. do, living c. prefer to, job d. do, life

A: ___ **16.** No, I think ___ a farmer ___ the hardest job.

a. been, is b. be, can c. being, is d. work as, does

Answers on page 96

Lesson 17: Names

імена

Learn the words

1. John
Джон

2. Matthew
Метью

3. Jason
Джейсон

4. Helen
Хелен

5. Mary
Мері

6. Kevin
Кевін

7. Tom
Том

8. Emily
Емілі

9. Jessica
Джессіка

10. Susan
Сьюзен

Learn the verb

call – calling – called – called дзвонити

I'll **call** Helen this evening.

I'm **calling** Helen now.

I **called** Helen last night.

I've **called** Helen today.

Learn the phrasal verb

Talk to

Meaning: To have a conversation with someone.

I was talking to Emily today.

Words: Write the missing letters

1. _o_n
2. _a_the_
3. _a_on
4. _ele_
5. _a_y

6. _e_i_
7. _o_
8. _mi_y
9. _e_si_a
10. _u_a_

Verbs: Past, Present or Future?

1. I have mistakenly been calling him "Tom" instead of "John".
☐ Past ☐ Present ☐ Future

2. Will you call Helen after you call Jason?
☐ Past ☐ Present ☐ Future

3. Kevin called Mary last weekend to find out the correct time.
☐ Past ☐ Present ☐ Future

Phrasal Verbs: Unscramble the sentences

1. Helen / on / talk / to / We / always / the / weekend

_____

2. I / talked / about / to / haven't / Jason / yet / it

_____

3. Mary / time / me / talked / for / to / long / a / yesterday

_____

Sentence Pattern 1

Who were you talking to today?

I was talking to <u>John</u> today.

Were you talking to <u>Susan</u> today?

A: Yes, I was.

B: No, I was talking to <u>Matthew</u>.

Sentence Pattern 2

Who is going to meet you later?

<u>Helen</u> is going to meet me later.

Is <u>Tom</u> going to meet you later?

A: Yes, Tom's going to meet me later.

B: No, <u>Jessica</u>'s going to meet me later.

Sentence Pattern 3

What did your parents name your baby <u>brother</u>?

They named him <u>Kevin</u>.

Did your parents name your baby <u>sister</u> <u>Mary</u>?

A: Yes, they did.

B: No, they named her <u>Emily</u>.

Sentence Pattern 1

Who _____ you _____ to _____?

I _____ talking _____ _____ today.

_____ you _____ to _____ today?

A: Yes, _____ _____.

B: _____, I _____ talking _____ _____.

Sentence Pattern 2

Who _____ going _____ meet _____ later?

_____ is _____ to _____ me _____.

Is _____ _____ to _____ you later?

A: Yes, _____ going _____ meet _____ later.

B: _____, Kevin's _____ to _____ me _____.

Sentence Pattern 3

What _____ your _____ name _____ baby _____?

They _____ her _____.

Did _____ parents _____ your _____ brother _____?

A: Yes, _____ _____.

B: No, _____ named _____ _____.

Lesson 18: More places

додаткові місця

Learn the words

1. **the library**
   бібліотека
2. **school**
   школа
3. **the hospital**
   лікарня
4. **the train station**
   залізнична станція
5. **the police station**
   міліція

6. **the office**
   офіс
7. **the factory**
   фабрика, завод
8. **the clinic**
   поліклініка
9. **the bus stop**
   автобусна зупинка
10. **the fire station**
    пожежне депо

Learn the verb

go – going – went – gone йти

We **go** to the library on Saturdays.

We're **going** to the library now.

We **went** to the library last Saturday.

We will have **gone** to the library by Saturday.

Learn the phrasal verb

Get back

Meaning: To return from a location.

She'll get back from the office by half past six.

Words: Write the vowels

1. l_br_r_
2. sch_ _l
3. h_sp_t_l
4. tr_ _n st_t_ _n
5. p_l_c_ st_t_ _n

6. _ff_c_
7. f_ct_r_
8. cl_n_c
9. b_s st_p
10. f_r_ st_t_ _n

Verbs: Which verb?

1. We haven't _____ to the train station in a long time.

2. He _____ to school much earlier than everyone else each day.

3. They will be _____ to the library before the office.

4. My uncle _____ to the fire station yesterday.

Phrasal Verbs: Unscramble the sentences

1. late / the / back / got / I / factory / very / from

_____

2. the / getting / back / They're / soon / office / from

_____

3. back / gotten / She / the / from / hasn't / library / yet

_____

Sentence Pattern 1

What time will he get back from <u>the hospital</u>?

He'll get back from the hospital by half past <u>two</u>.

Will she get back from <u>the office</u> by half past <u>six</u>?

A: Yes, she'll get back by then.

B: No, she'll get back later than half past six.

Sentence Pattern 2

Where have you been this week?

I've been to <u>the hospital</u> this week.

Have you been to <u>the factory</u> this week?

A: Yes, I have.

B: No, I haven't been there this week.

Sentence Pattern 3

When can you take <u>Kevin</u> to <u>the hospital</u>?

I can take him to <u>the hospital</u> now.

Can you take <u>Jessica</u> to <u>school</u> now?

A: Yes, I can.

B: No, I don't have time right now.

Sentence Pattern 1

What _____ will she _____ back _____ _____?

_____ get _____ _____ school by _____ past _____.

Will he _____ _____ from the _____ by half _____ four?

A: _____, he'll _____ back _____ then.

B: No, _____ get back _____ than _____ past _____.

Sentence Pattern 2

Where _____ you _____ this _____?

_____ been _____ the fire _____ this _____.

_____ you _____ to the _____ this _____?

A: _____, I _____.

B: No, I _____ been _____ _____ week.

Sentence Pattern 3

_____ can you _____ _____ to the _____ station?

I _____ take _____ to the train _____ now.

_____ you _____ Susan to the _____ stop _____?

A: Yes, _____ _____.

B: _____, I _____ have _____ right _____.

Lesson 19: Meats

м'ясо

Learn the words

1. **beef**
   яловичина
2. **pork**
   свинина
3. **bacon**
   бекон
4. **fish**
   риба
5. **salami**
   салямі

6. **chicken**
   курятина
7. **lamb**
   баранина
8. **ham**
   шинка
9. **sausage**
   ковбаса
10. **shrimp**
    креветки

Learn the verb

eat – eating – ate – eaten їсти

They **eat** chicken once a week.

They have been **eating** chicken once a week.

They **ate** chicken once a week.

They had **eaten** chicken once a week.

Learn the phrasal verb

Prepare for

Meaning: To get ready for something.

He has prepared some chicken for the barbecue.

Words: Unscramble the words

1. ccnkehi _____   6. ocbna _____

2. phirsm _____   7. efbe _____

3. abml _____   8. liamsa _____

4. asuegas _____   9. rokp _____

5. mha _____   10. sfhi _____

Verbs: ing or no ing?

1. He had never ____ shrimp before last week. ☐ eating ☐ eaten

2. My family often ____ fish for dinner . ☐ eating ☐ eats

3. We ____ beef for lunch last time. ☐ eating ☐ ate

4. They've been ____ a lot of chicken recently. ☐ eat ☐ eating

5. ____ too much meat can be unhealthy. ☐ Eat ☐ Eating

Phrasal Verbs: Unscramble the sentences

1. for / They / shrimp / a / of / prepared / lot / the / party

_____

2. some / their / He / breakfast / for / bacon / prepared

_____

3. chicken / some / everyone / She's / sandwiches / preparing / for

_____

Sentence Pattern 1

What has your <u>mother</u> prepared for the barbecue?

She has prepared some <u>beef</u> for the barbecue.

Has your <u>uncle</u> prepared some <u>lamb</u> for the barbecue?

A: Yes, he has.

B: No, he's prepared some <u>chicken</u>.

Sentence Pattern 2

What do you usually eat for <u>dinner</u>?

We usually eat <u>fish</u> or <u>pork</u> for dinner.

Do you usually eat <u>bacon</u> for <u>breakfast</u>?

A: Yes, we do.

B: No, we usually eat <u>ham</u> for breakfast.

Sentence Pattern 3

How are you going to cook the <u>sausage</u>?

I'm going to cook the <u>sausage</u> in the <u>pan</u>.

Are you going to cook the <u>lamb</u> in the <u>oven</u>?

A: Yes, I am.

B: No, I'm going to cook it in the pan.

Sentence Pattern 1

What _____ your _____ prepared _____ the _____?

She has _____ some _____ for _____ barbecue.

Has _____ brother _____ some _____ for the _____?

A: Yes, _____ _____.

B: _____, he's prepared _____ _____.

Sentence Pattern 2

What _____ you _____ eat for _____?

We _____ eat _____ _____ salami _____ breakfast.

_____ you usually _____ ham _____ dinner?

A: _____, we _____.

B: No, _____ usually eat _____ for _____.

Sentence Pattern 3

How _____ you _____ to _____ the _____?

I'm going _____ cook _____ fish _____ the _____.

Are you _____ to _____ the _____ in the _____?

A: Yes, _____ _____.

B: _____, I'm _____ to _____ it in _____ pan.

Lesson 20: Vegetables

овочі

Learn the words

1. **pumpkin**
   гарбуз
2. **potato**
   картопля
3. **carrot**
   морква
4. **asparagus**
   спаржа
5. **broccoli**
   брокколі

6. **corn**
   кукурудза
7. **cabbage**
   капуста
8. **spinach**
   шпинат
9. **mushroom**
   гриб
10. **onion**
    цибуля

Learn the verb

cook – cooking – cooked – cooked готувати

My aunt **cooks** some broccoli for us.

My aunt is **cooking** some broccoli for us.

My aunt **cooked** some broccoli for us.

My aunt has **cooked** some broccoli for us.

Learn the phrasal verb

Be good for

Meaning: To benefit something in a positive way.

I heard mushroom is good for your health.

Words: Complete the words

1. p_____o

2. b_____i

3. c_____t

4. a_____s

5. p_____n

6. c_____e

7. o_____n

8. s_____h

9. m_____m

10. c_____n

Verbs: Find the mistake

1. At what time will you cooking the broccoli for dinner? **Correct:** _____

2. I've never cook asparagus, so I don't know how to. **Correct:** _____

3. The cook didn't cooked the spinach very well. **Correct:** _____

4. Are you cook the corn and carrot together? **Correct:** _____

5. My friend usually cooking a really good pumpkin soup. **Correct:** _____

Phrasal Verbs: Unscramble the sentences

1. is / Onion / good / putting / for / in / soup

_____

2. for / is / Pumpkin / good / health / really / your

_____

3. adding / is / Spinach / for / to / good / salads

_____

Sentence Pattern 1

Why are you eating more <u>mushroom</u>?

I heard mushroom is good for your health.

Is <u>corn</u> good for your health?

A: Yes, it certainly is.

B: I'm not exactly sure.

Sentence Pattern 2

What vegetable would you rather eat tonight?

I'd rather eat <u>cabbage</u> tonight.

Would you rather eat <u>asparagus</u> tonight?

A: Yes, I would.

B: No, I'd rather eat <u>pumpkin</u>.

Sentence Pattern 3

How have you been eating healthier?

Lately, I've been eating more <u>broccoli</u>.

Have you been eating healthier lately?

A: Yes, I've been eating more <u>spinach</u>.

B: No, but I want to eat healthier.

Sentence Pattern 1

Why _____ you _____ more _____?

I _____ pumpkin is _____ for _____ health.

Is _____ good _____ your _____?

A: _____, it _____ is.

B: I'm _____ exactly _____.

Sentence Pattern 2

What _____ would _____ rather _____ tonight?

I'd _____ eat _____ _____.

_____ you _____ eat _____ tonight?

A: Yes, _____ _____.

B: No, _____ rather _____ potato.

Sentence Pattern 3

How _____ you _____ eating _____?

_____, I've _____ eating _____ _____.

Have _____ been _____ healthier _____?

A: Yes, _____ _____ eating more _____.

B: No, _____ I _____ _____ eat _____.

Write the answer next to the letter "A"

A: ___ **1.** She said that she's ___ Jason ___.

a. calling, now   b. call, today   c. calls, this evening   d. called, last night

A: ___ **2.** Were you ___ to Kim today? No, I was talking ___ Mary.

a. talked, for   b. talk, to   c. talks, at   d. talking, to

A: ___ **3.** No, ___ going to meet me ___.

a. John, now   b. John is, already   c. John's, later   d. John's, lately

A: ___ **4.** ___ your parents ___ your baby brother Jason?

a. Have, call   b. Did, name   c. What, named   d. Do, called

A: ___ **5.** They ___ have been ___ to the factory for two years by then.

a. are, go   b. will, going   c. would, went   d. can, gone

A: ___ **6.** She'll get back from the police station ___ half ___ one.

a. at, to   b. later, past   c. by, past   d. lately, o'clock

A: ___ **7.** Have you been ___ the clinic this week? Yes, I ___.

a. at, been   b. to, have   c. by, gone   d. for, go

A: ___ **8.** Can you ___ Tom to the train station now? Yes, I ___.

a. take, can   b. taking, could   c. take, take   d. taken, can

A: ___ **9.** We ___ never ___ salami before today.

a. has, ate   b. are, eat   c. had, eaten   d. have, eating

A: ___ **10.** ___ your father prepared some sausage ___ the barbecue?

a. Has, for   b. Did, for   c. Have, in   d. Is, during

A: ___ **11.** We usually ___ ham ___ shrimp for dinner.

a. eating, and   b. ate, during   c. eat, or   d. eaten, on

A: ___ **12.** ___ you going to cook the chicken ___ the pan? Yes, I am.

a. How, on   b. Are, in   c. Have, by   d. Are, by

A: ___ **13.** My brother always ___ some onion ___ lunch.

a. cooking, at   b. cooked, by   c. cook, during   d. cooks, for

A: ___ **14.** I heard asparagus ___ good ___ your health.

a. are, by   b. can, at   c. is, for   d. have, on

A: ___ **15.** Would you ___ eat pumpkin tonight? Yes, I ___.

a. like to, like   b. prefer, would   c. rather, rather   d. rather, would

A: ___ **16.** ___, I've ___ eating more potato.

a. Later, been   b. This time, be   c. Lately, been   d. Today, being

Answers on page 96

Answers

Test 1 Test
1. c   2. a   3. c   4. b   5. b   6. d   7. a   8. d   9. b   10. a 11. c 12. d 13. c 14. a
15. c 16. d

Test 2 Test
1. d   2. a   3. a   4. b   5. c   6. d   7. b   8. d   9. b   10. c 11. c 12. d 13. d 14. b
15. d 16. a

Test 3 Test
1. b   2. d   3. b   4. a   5. d   6. c   7. a   8. c   9. b   10. a 11. c 12. b 13. c 14. b
15. a 16. b

Test 4 Test
1. b   2. c   3. c   4. b   5. b   6. d   7. a   8. d   9. b   10. b 11. c 12. d 13. a 14. c
15. b 16. c

Test 5 Test
1. a   2. d   3. c   4. b   5. b   6. c   7. b   8. a   9. c   10. a 11. c 12. b 13. d 14. c
15. d 16. c

Preston Lee's other great books!

Preston Lee's Beginner English

Preston Lee's Beginner English For Ukrainian Speakers (44 Lessons)

Preston Lee's Beginner English Lesson 1 – 60 For Ukrainian Speakers

Preston Lee's Beginner English Lesson 1 – 80 For Ukrainian Speakers

Preston Lee's Beginner English 100 Lessons For Ukrainian Speakers

- ### Preston Lee's Beginner English 20 Lesson Series

Preston Lee's Beginner English Lesson 1 – 20 For Ukrainian Speakers

Preston Lee's Beginner English Lesson 21 – 40 For Ukrainian Speakers

Preston Lee's Beginner English Lesson 41 – 60 For Ukrainian Speakers

Preston Lee's Beginner English Lesson 61 – 80 For Ukrainian Speakers

Preston Lee's Intermediate English

Preston Lee's Intermediate English Lesson 1 – 40 For Ukrainian Speakers

- ### Preston Lee's Intermediate English 20 Lesson Series

Preston Lee's Intermediate English Lesson 1 – 20 For Ukrainian Speakers

Preston Lee's Intermediate English Lesson 21 – 40 For Ukrainian Speakers

Preston Lee's Conversation English

Preston Lee's Conversation English Lesson 1 – 40 For Ukrainian Speakers

Preston Lee's Conversation English Lesson 1 – 60 For Ukrainian Speakers

Preston Lee's Conversation English 100 Lessons For Ukrainian Speakers

- ### Preston Lee's Conversation English 20 Lesson Series

Preston Lee's Conversation English Lesson 1 – 20 For Ukrainian Speakers

Preston Lee's Conversation English Lesson 21 – 40 For Ukrainian Speakers

Preston Lee's Conversation English Lesson 41 – 60 For Ukrainian Speakers

Preston Lee's Read & Write English

Preston Lee's Read & Write English Lesson 1 – 40 For Ukrainian Speakers

Preston Lee's Read & Write English Lesson 1 – 60 For Ukrainian Speakers

- ### Preston Lee's Read & Write English 20 Lesson Series

Preston Lee's Read & Write English Lesson 1 – 20 For Ukrainian Speakers

Preston Lee's Read & Write English Lesson 21 – 40 For Ukrainian Speakers

Preston Lee's Read & Write English Lesson 41 – 60 For Ukrainian Speakers

Preston Lee's Beginner English Words

Preston Lee's Beginner English 500 Words For Ukrainian Speakers

Preston Lee's Beginner English 800 Words For Ukrainian Speakers

Preston Lee's Beginner English 1000 Words For Ukrainian Speakers

Printed in Great Britain
by Amazon

85707513R10059